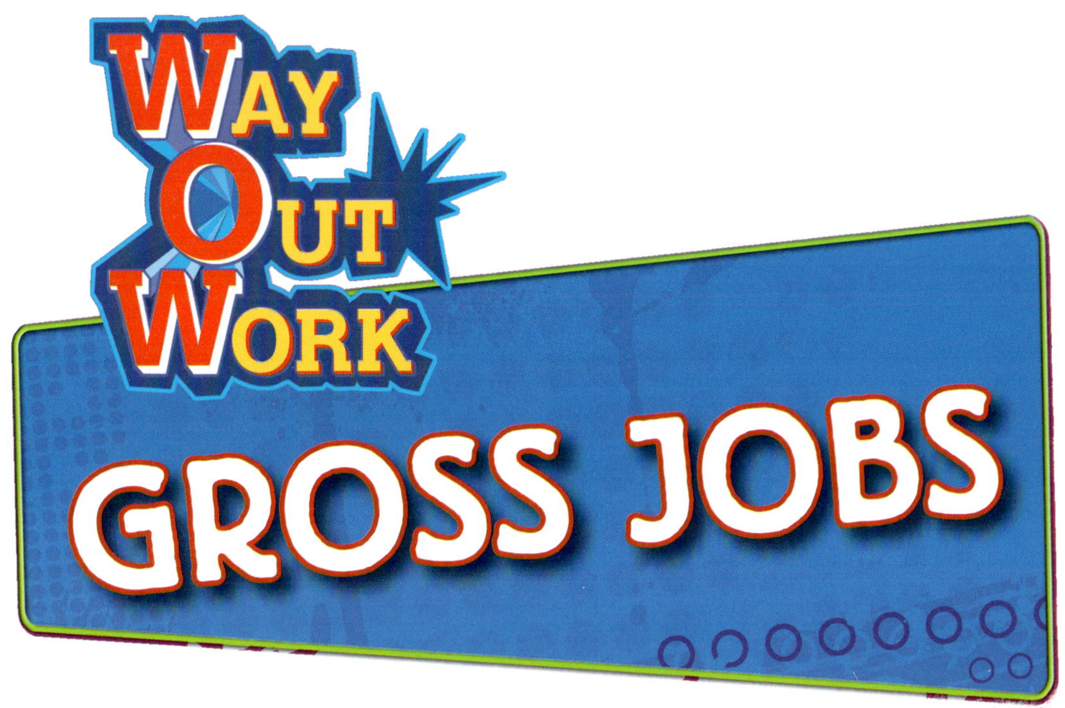

Diane Lindsey Reeves

Ferguson
An imprint of Infobase Publishing

Acknowledgements

Special thanks to Lyle Estill, Michael L. Fox, Judith Gordon, and Kathy Reichs for sharing the secrets of their awesome gross jobs! Thanks also to Joy Strickland, who assisted in researching and writing this book.

Way Out Work: Gross Jobs

Ferguson
An imprint of Infobase Publishing
132 West 31st Street
New York, NY 10001

Library of Congress Cataloging-in-Publication Data
Reeves, Diane Lindsey, 1959-
Gross jobs / Diane Lindsey Reeves.—1st ed.
p. cm.—(Way out work)
Includes index.
ISBN-13: 978-1-60413-131-4 (hbk : alk. paper)
ISBN-10: 1-60413-131-4 (hbk : alk. paper) 1. Job descriptions—Juvenile literature. 2. Occupations—Juvenile literature. 3. Vocational guidance—Juvenile literature. I. Title.
HF5381.2.R443 2009
331.702—dc22
2009008227

Ferguson books are available at special discounts when purchased in bulk quantities for businesses, associations, institutions, or sales promotions. Please call our Special Sales Department in New York at (212) 967-8800 or (800) 322-8755.

You can find Ferguson on the World Wide Web at http://www.fergpubco.com

Text design by Erika K. Arroyo
Cover design by Jooyoung An

Printed in the United States of America

Bang MSRF 10 9 8 7 6 5 4 3 2 1

This book is printed on acid-free paper.

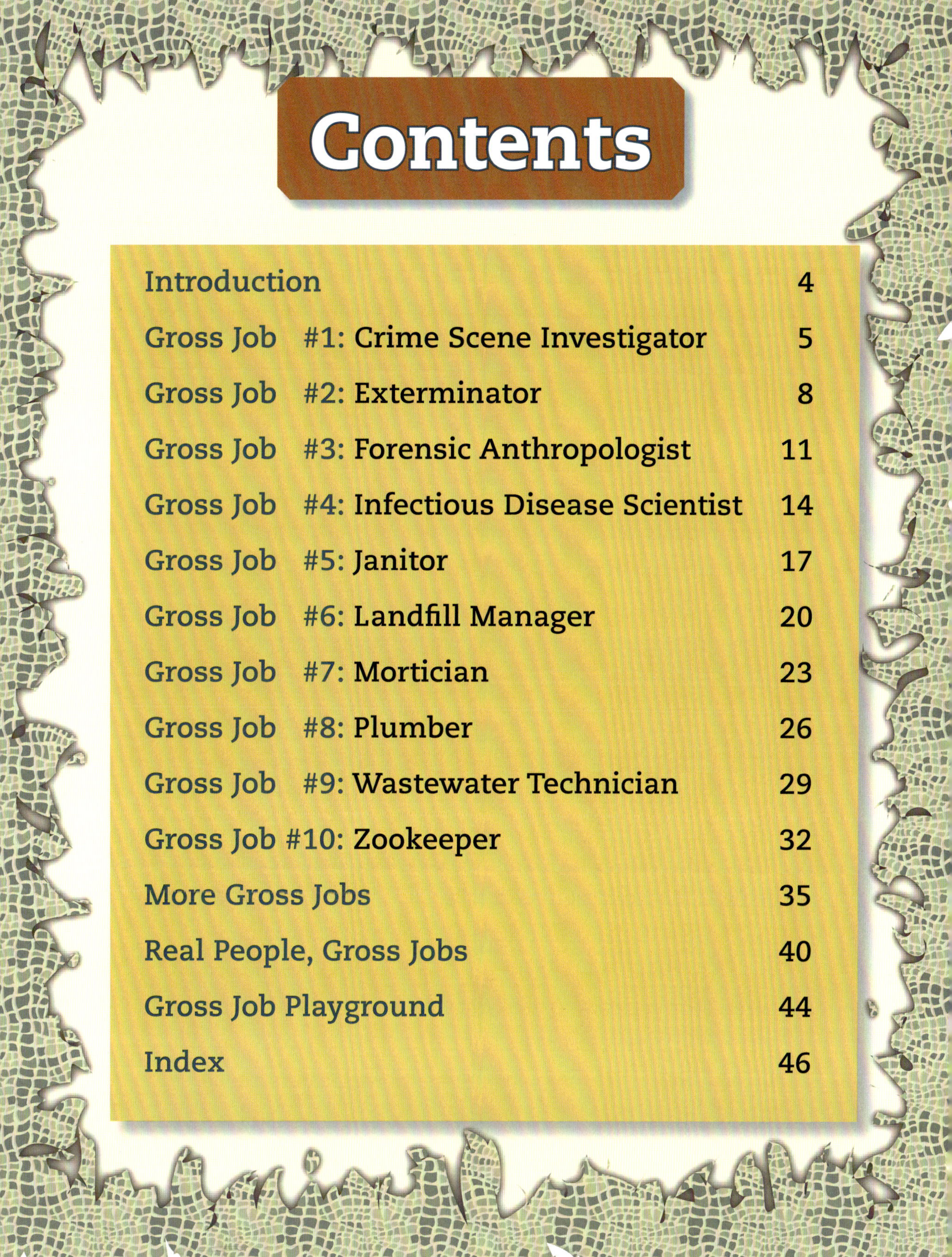

Contents

Introduction

They clean up your messes. They take out your trash. They make sure you have safe drinking water. They even make you look good in the very worst of circumstances. In short, they do countless things for you that, given the choice, you'd probably rather not do yourself. And, no, *they* aren't your parents.

Who are these people and why hasn't the world given them medals yet? They are the janitors, the wastewater engineers, the trash collectors, and other unsung heroes who do the dirty work that keeps the world clean and safe. They bravely tackle tasks that would make most people gag. Blood and guts. Corpses and carcasses. Animals and insects. Stinky, dirty stuff. These people routinely work with things that would totally gross you out.

What do these people do? And why in the world do they do what they do? Answers to these questions and more are coming your way as you start reading about some of the world's grossest jobs.

The first 10 chapters include several interesting features to get you thinking about these jobs in new and unexpected ways. Then get ready to freak out with more gross job ideas, and make sure you stop by to read what real people have to say about what their jobs are really like. Plan to spend a little time at the end of the book, where you can find out once and for all if you've got the guts it takes to do what these people do.

Gross Job #1

Crime Scene Investigator

Police crime scene investigators inspect the area outside the British Consulate offices in Manhattan after a small explosive device was detonated on the sidewalk. *Seth Wenig/ Reuters/Landov*

Blood and guts are everywhere. The room is a total disaster, with toppled furniture and torn curtains. Drawers are askew and papers are strewn all over the floor. Menacing shards of glass from a broken window are scattered across the carpet. You don't have to be Nancy Drew or one of the Hardy Boys to realize that something very bad has happened here. If you are a crime scene investigator, it's your job to gather evidence that will help police detectives find out what happened. Do your job well and the evidence you collect may be the very thing that cracks the case.

Evidence is everywhere! And since you don't know yet which clues are important and which aren't, you have to treat everything with the

What Do You Think?
Why do you think crime scene investigators take a ton of pictures at crime scenes?

utmost care. Which is why you go over the scene inch by inch, carefully taking photographs of every angle, gathering even the tiniest clues, taking time to bag them and document exactly where you found them. After all, sometimes all it takes is a single strand of hair to solve a crime! You dust the room for fingerprints, hoping that the criminal left his or her one-of-a-kind "calling card" somewhere in the room.

Crime scene investigators rely on a variety of special tools to do their jobs. Some tools are high tech like the Laser Scaling and Measurement Device for Photographic Images (LSMDPI), originally designed by NASA engineers to be used in space missions. Crime scene investigators now use this device to take incredibly precise photographs of crime scene evidence such as blood splatters. Of course, technology can't top some low-tech tools like axes and shovels when crime scene investigators need to dig for evidence.

As you can probably imagine, a crime scene is generally not a pretty sight. It takes time, but crime scene investigators eventually learn to look past the gore so that they can get down to the business of solving crimes. And, yes, in case you are wondering, sometimes the "evidence" includes a dead body. When

WOW!

Good news! The Bureau of Justice reports that violent crime has been decreasing in the United States since 1994, and it reached its lowest point ever in 2005.

There's nothing you like better than a good mystery.

You always take shortcuts to finish your homework faster.

that's the case, investigators examine the victim for any obvious clues. Then they work closely with forensic pathologists, who run in-depth tests and perform autopsies, which provide even more clues about the cause of death.

Gathering evidence is just the first part of this process. Once they get the evidence back to their labs, crime scene investigators have to piece together clues and figure out what it all means. This often involves sending evidence to other experts for special testing that can take a long time to complete. Crime scene investigators consider it good news when they have to go to court to testify about a case because it means that police were able to use their evidence to nab a suspect.

Go Online to Find Out More!

Solve your own crime scene at http://www.mysterynet.com/see.

Gross Job #2 Exterminator

An exterminator sprays insecticide outside an office building. *Kyoko Hamada/Getty Images*

You know the popular saying, "You've got ants in your pants"? Want to hear something even worse? Try ants in your house! Crawling around your cupboards, messing around in your sock drawer, eating up all of your favorite snacks...Could there be anything grosser? As a matter of fact, there is. How would you like to have roaches (ick!), spiders (ugh!), or, worst of all, rats (yikes!) running around your house?

Lucky for you (and for millions of other people with pest-infested homes), here comes an exterminator to the rescue. Exterminators get rid

of unwanted creatures, also known as "pests," in people's homes and businesses. Exterminators encounter some of the creepiest creatures imaginable in order to protect people from diseases carried by insects and rodents.

To do their job, exterminators have to know what they are up against. For instance, black widow spiders are poisonous (watch out, they bite!), while jumping spiders can hop up to 25 times their own body length (be prepared for them to give you a run for your money!). Knowing how various pests operate and what kind of damage they can do to human habitats helps exterminators determine the best way to get rid of them.

Since most pests know better than to come out and say "hi" when an exterminator comes to visit, the exterminator often has to get down and dirty trying to find them—sometimes crawling under houses or poking around dusty attics to track them

What Do You Think?

Father and son Jonathan and Steven Frisch invented a humane rat trap that uses herbs to lull rodents to sleep so people can remove them from their homes and release them somewhere else without killing them. Is this a good pest control situation? Why or why not?

WOW!

According to the World Health Organization, the mosquito is the most notorious of all insects for spreading deadly diseases like malaria, dengue fever, and yellow fever.

You've never met an insect you didn't like to squish!

You scream every time you see a spider.

down. Which, of course, means that exterminators often get a little closer to creepy critters than most people would prefer. But one person's gross-out is just another day on the job for an experienced exterminator.

Finding the pests is just the first step. An exterminator isn't finished until he or she figures out how to make them leave. But the exterminator has a lot of options—some more humane than others. Sometimes sealing up the places where critters sneak into the house will do the trick. Other times more drastic actions like using fumigants or poisonous gases are necessary. In cases where tiny insects called termites have totally infested a house, it sometimes becomes necessary for the people to evacuate so that the exterminator can put a gigantic tent around the house and fill it with powerful fumigants that get rid of the wood-eating critters. Who knew that tiny little bugs could literally eat people out of house and home!

The art of extermination has even gone high tech. One of the most popular devices is a microchip implanted in a bait station. When termites get too close, the chip signals to the exterminator that pests are inside the house and that it's time to do something about it. This technology makes the process more precise and efficient. One tiny microchip for exterminators, millions of clean houses for mankind!

Go Online to Find Out More!

Discover what kind of pests may be lurking in your backyard at http://pestworldforkids.org.

Gross Job #3

Forensic Anthropologist

A forensic anthropologist sets up sonar technology to detect the location of buried human remains. *Vanderlei Almeida/AFP/Getty Images*

It's Monday morning and you want to get an early start at work. No one else has arrived yet so you unlock the door, turn on the lights, and—what in the world?—find a pile of human bones lying on the examination table in your laboratory. Who is this person? What happened to him or her? Is this some sort of scary Halloween trick?

No, it's not a trick. Your job as a forensic anthropologist is to find out who this person is and how he or she died. The work requires you to be part scientist and part detective. As a scientist, you will use an impressive knowledge of the human skeleton to uncover clues about the person's physical characteristics. As a detective, you will piece together evidence to link these bones with a specific person. After all, police depend on you to help identify people whose

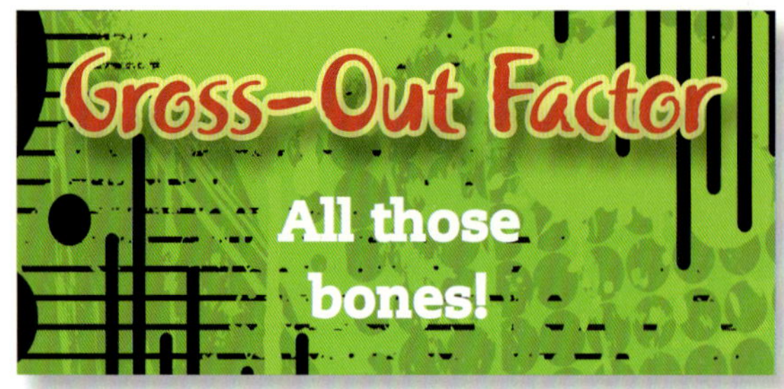

What Do You Think?
Forensic pathologists perform autopsies on dead human bodies, while forensic anthropologists work with only the bones of dead people. Which task would gross you out the most? Why?

remains are so badly decomposed—due to time, exposure to weather, fire, or criminal violence—that they cannot be recognized by other means.

So you scrub up, put on your protective work clothes, and get down to business. Before you are finished, you will run all kinds of sophisticated tests that will help you determine the person's gender, age, height, ethnic background, approximate time of death, and other distinguishing characteristics. In some cases you may compare DNA samples from the victim with other evidence.

Once you've gathered all those physical clues, the sleuthing begins. You know a lot about what this person was (male or female, tall or short, black or white...). Now you want to find out who the victim was. You start by looking at missing person reports about people with similar characteristics who disappeared around the time that the victim died. You talk with detectives and other witnesses who may have useful information. Little by little, a story begins to emerge.

All of this information, test results, and other data are eventually com-

WOW!

Did you know that your thighbone is stronger than concrete? Yes, the thighbone, or femur, is the strongest bone in the body and, get this, it's hollow!

You dig history and science.

You get nightmares just thinking about touching a real human skeleton.

piled into a very thorough report that law enforcement officers and other officials can use to notify the victim's loved ones, pursue criminal investigations, or tie up other loose ends so that the victim can finally rest in peace.

Of course, not all of forensic anthropology cases are criminal in nature. It isn't unusual for construction workers to find human bones when excavating new construction sites. In these situations, it is unlikely that a forensic anthropologist would be able to identify a specific person. Instead, they might gather evidence to determine how old the bones are and if the construction workers have happened upon a site with historic significance, like a Native American burial ground or Civil War cemetery. No matter the end result, forensic anthropologists work to provide a voice for people who can no longer speak for themselves.

Go Online to Find Out More!

You'll wonder no more about what forensic scientists do after visiting http://www.iwaswondering.org/diane_homepage.html.

Gross Job #4

Infectious Disease Scientist

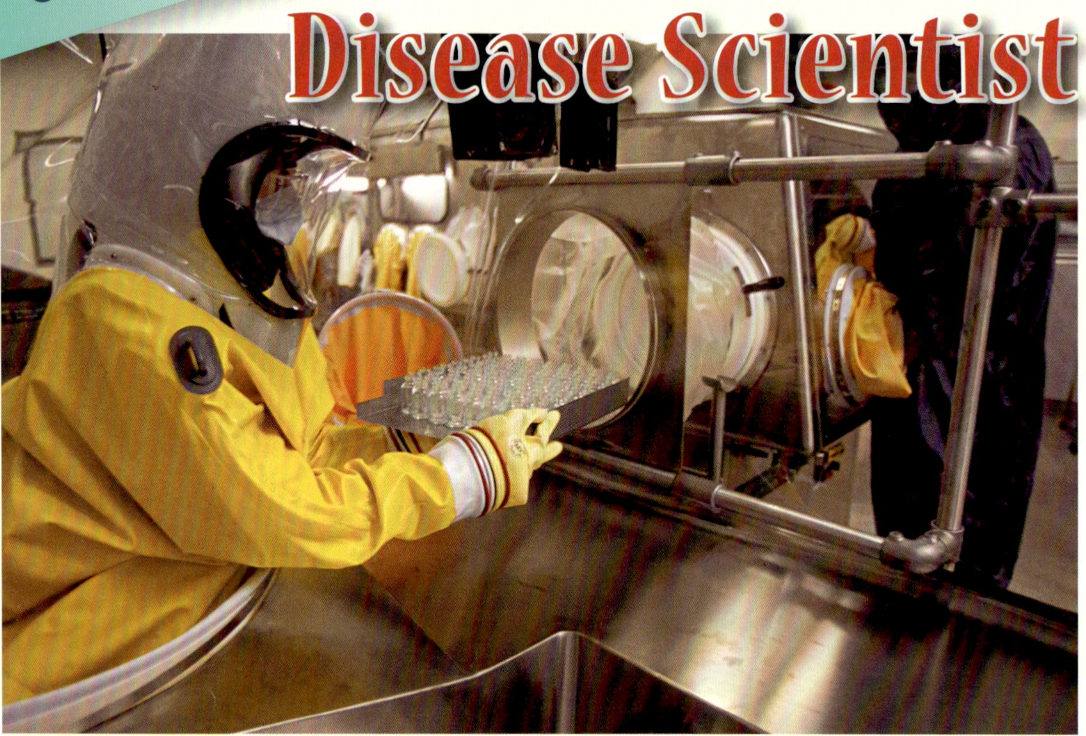

Infectious disease scientists prepare to manufacture the smallpox virus in their lab. *Karen Kasmauski/Corbis*

Uh-oh, a killer flu bug is on the loose! It's 1918 and the disease is killing millions of people all over the world. It starts with the usual flu-like symptoms of body aches, cough, and fever—then zaps its victims with fatal bouts of pneumonia and other complications. The Spanish Flu epidemic was the deadliest plague in history and posed one of the greatest challenges ever faced by the scientists who make it their job to protect the world from infectious disease disasters.

These days, infectious disease scientists have their hands full investigating new (and annoyingly persistent) germs. Their job is to figure out ways to either prevent these germs from hurting people or to develop medicines and other treatments to

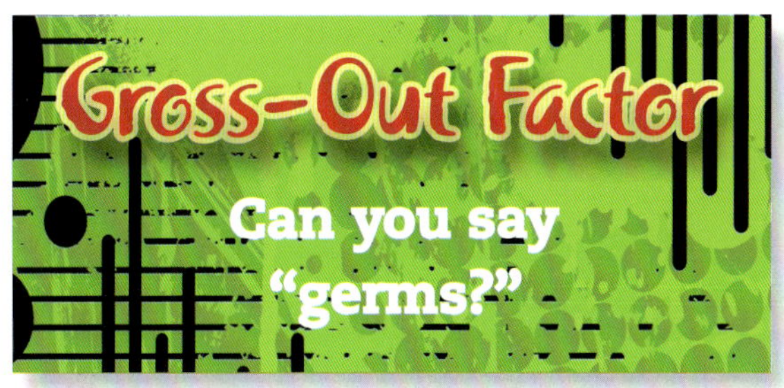

help people who have already been infected. Sometimes their quest for a disease-free world can take them far from home to places like the Amazon and the Sahara to track down emerging diseases. They may even bring back samples of villainous germs to their labs so that they can conduct research about how they do their dastardly damage.

Infectious disease researchers have to go through years of training before they are ready to get face-to-face with AIDs, influenza, typhus, or any other modern disease challenges. After completing several years of college and medical school, these doctors go through three more years of specialized training in infectious diseases.

Unfortunately, nature's bad guys aren't the only culprits these scientists have to fight. Some also monitor diseases that might be used as weapons in war. Such diseases are known as "bioterrorism threats" and include dangers like anthrax (spread as a white powder that can cause lung, skin, and other infections) or smallpox (a disease that causes high fever and sores). In October 2001 a terrorist mailed envelopes containing anthrax

What Do You Think?

Washing your hands is one of the most effective ways to prevent the spread of infectious diseases. Why do you think this is true?

WOW!

There are four main types of germs: bacteria, viruses, fungi, and protozoa.

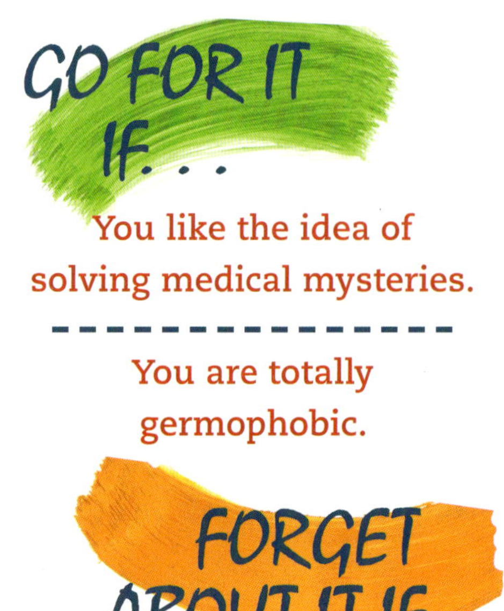

to people in New York, Florida, and Washington, D.C. The attack could have made thousands of people sick, but infectious disease scientists and many law enforcement professionals quickly got involved to protect the public.

Other infectious disease scientists work in areas where there has been a natural disaster to help prevent the spread of diseases caused by unclean water supplies and other problems. This was certainly the case when Hurricane Katrina wreaked havoc on the Gulf Coast in 2005. Still other infectious disease scientists work internationally with developing regions like Africa, where health care options are limited and there is a high risk of disease.

Getting up close and personal with dangerous bacteria and parasites is a routine part of the infectious disease scientist's job. Their willingness to risk these gross (and often dangerous) encounters often results in new medical discoveries that save millions of lives every year.

Go Online to Find Out More!

Investigate some infectious diseases at http://www.diseasedetectives.org.

Gross Job #5

Janitor

A janitor shampoos the carpet in an office. *Mark E. Gibson at CLM/Corbis Outline*

It's five minutes before your shift begins. You punch the time clock and dash down the hall to your boss's office to get your job assignments for the night. She hands you a clipboard with a list of tasks: Clean all bathrooms, empty trashcans in all offices, and vacuum all floors. You have to pinch yourself when the fact that there are 20 stinky bathrooms, more than 100 overflowing trashcans, and what seems like miles of dirty floors stretching out in front of you finally sinks in. Surely this is just a bad dream! There must be a mistake! Have you died and ended up in a place where endless chores are your eternal punishment?

Nope, it's not a dream. It's not a mistake. And, you'll be glad to know that you are still alive and kicking. You are a janitor, and it's your job to

clean people's offices and other public places after everyone else has gone home for the night. It's a big job—one that requires a lot of organization, attention to detail, and plenty of good old-fashioned elbow grease.

Don't even think about not doing a good job. An icky work environment is a surefire way to stop any business in its tracks. Unfortunately for you in this fictional account and to real janitors everywhere, this is a job that often goes unnoticed unless it's not done right. Businesses, schools, hospitals, restaurants, and all the places common in a civilized society depend on janitors and other types of cleaning professionals to keep things, well, civilized. In some cases, like hospital surgery rooms and intensive care wards, doing the job well can literally be a matter of life or death. In those situations, "almost clean" just doesn't cut it and can endanger patients with exposure to germs.

Bet you didn't know that the word "janitor" comes from the Latin term "janus" and means "doorkeeper." Depending on their responsibilities, janitors are sometimes called cus-

What Do You Think?

If you had no other choice, which would you rather clean: a baseball stadium after the last game of a World Series or a hospital intensive care unit for newborns? How would the two experiences be different?

WOW!

In case you've ever wondered, the average person uses the bathroom 2,500 times a year. That's about six to eight times a day.

todians, sanitation supervisors, or domestic engineers. Regardless of the title, this job typically involves cleaning everything from windows to washrooms. It may also involve fixing things and maintaining facilities—changing lightbulbs, painting dingy walls, and other tasks that keep buildings in tip-top shape.

This is not a job for wimps. It's physically demanding and requires an honest-to-goodness appreciation of a job well done. Next time you find yourself in need of a public restroom or enjoying a meal at a restaurant, remember the people whose job it is to keep it clean!

You are a clean freak.

Your school locker is so messy it takes you longer to find your homework than it takes you to do it.

Go Online to Find Out More!

Have a little fun doing chores with the online games and charts found at http://www.handipoints.com.

Gross Job #6

Landfill Manager

Landfill managers watch a bulldozer lift trash at a recycling site. *Gil Cohen Magen/Reuters/Landov*

Did you know that the average person generates about 4.6 pounds of trash every day? Multiply that number by the 365 days in a year. Then multiply that number by the total number of students in your class at school. Hmmm...That's a lot of trash, isn't it?

If you were to add the trash generated by you and your classmates with the rest of your fellow U.S. citizens, you'd come up with about 251 tons of "municipal solid waste," as it's officially called by the Environmental Protection Agency. This includes things people use and toss every day—things like product packaging, grass clippings, furniture, clothing, bottles, food scraps, newspapers, appliances, paint, and batteries. Wow! There are no ifs, ands, or buts about it—that's an enormous amount of trash!

So where does all that trash go? Most of it goes to one of 1,754 U.S. landfills. Increasing amounts of it, however, go into recycling programs where it finds new uses. In other words, "one man's trash becomes another man's treasure." Enterprising recyclers find golden opportunities in turning old newspapers into new newspaper, getting aluminum soda cans ready for refills, and even creating fashionable new fabrics out of used plastic bags.

Even so, there's still a lot of trash left over, and something has to be done with it. That's where the landfill manager comes in. He or she does pretty much what the job title implies: manage landfills. But make no mistake, the job is not as easy (or as smelly!) as it may seem. Experts know a lot more about how to safely dispose of trash than they did in the past. Done right, and by the extensive rules established by federal and state governments, landfills should be well organized, safe, and surprisingly tidy. Essentially, there's a place for everything and everything is in its place…recycled materials go here, toxic chemicals go there (where they can be safely disposed of), household debris goes over there, and old cars go somewhere else.

A landfill manager's job is a lot like running a very busy business.

What Do You Think?
If you joined in with only 25 percent of U.S. families to use 10 fewer plastic shopping bags a month, we would save over 2.5 BILLION bags a year. Are you up for the challenge?

WOW!
It can take up to about 500 years for a disposable diaper to decompose.

You want to help clean up the world.

You hate to take out the trash!

Trash collectors, consumers, and government regulators are people he or she deals with on a regular basis. There are people to manage, inspections to conduct, equipment to maintain, plans to be developed, and many reports to write.

Some landfill managers do such a good job that, once their landfills are full to capacity, others come in and turn what was once Mount Trashmore into beautiful parks, playgrounds, and greenways. Imagine that!

Go Online to Find Out More!

Get ready to go green at http://www.nrdc.org/GREENSQUAD.

Gross Job #7
Mortician

What do vampires and morticians have in common? They both go for the jugular vein! The difference, of course, is that vampires supposedly do it for a tasty snack, while morticians do it to prepare a dead body for burial. Morticians, also known as embalmers or funeral directors, do their work for two reasons: to give dignity to the dead and to bring comfort to the loved ones left behind. Their job is part creepy and part compassionate.

A funeral director prepares to show a selection of coffins to prospective clients.
Rainer Holz/zefa/Corbis

The creepy part involves emptying the corpse of all bodily fluids—its blood and guts, in other words. It's extra creepy when the person has died as a result of an accident or some sort of disfiguring injury. That's when a mortician uses things like wax, cotton, or plastic to rebuild or repair the remains so that the person looks as "normal" as possible. The creepiness doesn't end until the mortician has dressed the body (usually in the person's Sunday best clothes), given it a good manicure, applied makeup to give it a lifelike appearance, and styled its hair.

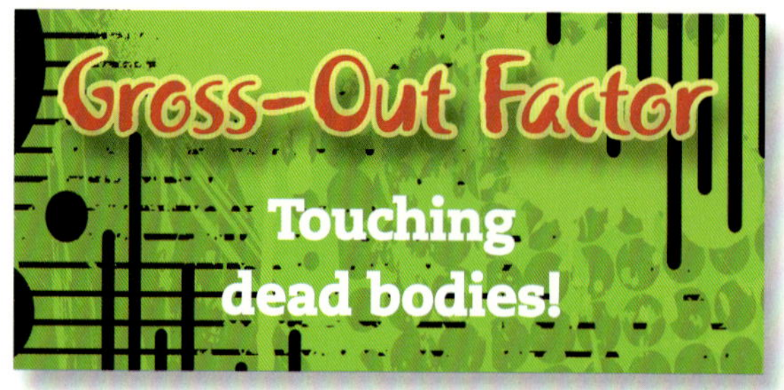

Sometimes the mortician gets help from a beauty technician, called a cosmetologist, for this part.

Creepiness gives way to compassion when dealing with the deceased person's family and friends. Dealing with the death of a loved one is never easy, but seeing that the deceased person looks familiar and at peace can make the grieving process a whole lot easier. Once the body is prepared, the mortician often assumes other duties as funeral director. Making sure that the funeral process is dignified and that the family and other guests are comfortable and well cared for are other ways that a mortician shows compassion.

In addition to being kind of creepy and very compassionate, this job is also part science—requiring knowledge of anatomy, microbiology, pathology, and chemistry—and part art—requiring good people skills and, in some cases, even a working knowledge of cosmetology. Of course, it helps to have a strong stomach too, and a sense of humor doesn't hurt. Morticians work for funeral homes, hospitals, medical schools, and morgues (places where bodies are held until they can be identified or until the cause of death can be determined).

What Do You Think?

What do you think is the most compassionate way to care for the remains of a deceased person: cremation or embalming for burial?

WOW!

There is no law that says a body must be embalmed.

You have a strong stomach and a soft heart.

You faint at the sight of blood.

Not just anyone gets to be a mortician. The job requires special training in mortuary science, an apprenticeship with an experienced mortician, and a state license earned after successfully completing a big test. Those considering this line of work in the future can rest assured of plenty of job opportunities because death, as they say, like taxes, is one of the only things in life that is certain.

Go Online to Find Out More!

If you think modern mortuary science is gross, just wait until you read about how the ancient Egyptians prepared mummies for burial at http://science.howstuffworks.com/mummy.htm.

Gross Job #8

Plumber

Plumbers install a kitchen sink. *Jim Craigmyle/Corbis*

You know it's going to be a bad day when you wake up early in the morning, head for the bathroom, do your business, flush, and, oops!—instead of going down the toilet, everything comes right back up! Unless you (or your parents) are extra handy with a plunger, this is a job for the experts. Yeah, right. As if there really is such a thing as a toilet expert.

Oh, but there is, and before you start snickering, you may want to look at how much they charge to fix your plugged-up commode! These experts are called plumbers and, according to the dictionary, they are people who install and repair piping, fixtures, appliances, and appurtenances in connection with the water supply, drainage systems, and septic systems both inside and outside buildings.

It may be hard to believe but indoor plumbing as we know it today is a

What Do You Think?
What's the weirdest thing you've ever flushed down a toilet?

fairly modern convenience. For a long time it was a luxury enjoyed only by the wealthy. But improper waste disposal is more than just gross; it can also be deadly. It wasn't until officials realized that poor sewage systems were causing serious outbreaks of diseases, like typhus and cholera, that indoor plumbing became regarded as a necessity. Of course, some rural homes in the United States still did not have indoor plumbing until well after the mid-1900s—relying on wells and springs for water and outhouses and chamber pots for bathrooms.

Plumbers don't just fix problems like backed-up toilets. They also install, maintain, and repair many different types of piping systems. Plumbers tend to focus on pipes that move water, waste, and gas throughout homes and commercial buildings. They are often responsible for setting up entire sanitation systems.

This means that not only do plumbers have to be good at using tools like wrenches, pumps, and pipe-cutters, but they also have to be good at math and reading blueprints. Installing pipes requires precise measurements and careful attention to create an efficient and effective system capable of moving clean water in and dirty water out. Patience and a knack for details are traits that come in handy in this line of work.

You don't mind getting your hands dirty.

You get queasy just smelling a baby's diaper.

Plumbing is one of those professions that most people either don't want to do (for obvious reasons!) or don't know how to do. Which is why plumbers often get paid big bucks to do other people's dirty work for them. Just think about it: What if your home's sewer system backed up and the worst kind of crud was oozing all over your basement floor? How much would it be worth to you to have someone else clean up the mess and fix the problem? Uh-huh. Now you know why a good plumber is often one of the most popular people in town!

Go Online to Find Out More!

Fix the leaks at Water Works at http://justkidsgames.com/play.php?WaterWorks.

Gross Job #9

Wastewater Technician

A wastewater technician hoses down a small dam at a wastewater treatment plant. *AP Photo/ Rich Pedroncelli*

Everybody does it—even movie stars and sports heroes. There's no doubt about it—even the president of the United States has to "go." When you stop and think about it, there's a whole lot of "going" going on! Have you ever wondered where all that "going" goes?

Quite frankly, the waste you eliminate has quite an adventure after it leaves your body (and so does the water you rinse down the drain). First, it runs through the plumbing systems in your house, school, or wherever you happen to be when you use the toilet, sink, or tub. Then it flows down into a seemingly endless maze of sewer pipes deep beneath the streets and makes its way to the nearest wastewater treatment facility—

which, incidentally, might be miles away. Once it arrives, wastewater technicians start doing their thing to clean the water and send it back into the world.

After all, there's only so much water available on earth. It just keeps coming and going through the endless circle of evaporation, condensation, precipitation, and collection known as the water cycle. Did you realize that the water you drink from your faucets is the same water that dinosaurs slurped up from rivers and lakes?

Which is why it's very important that we take good care of the water and keep it clean. When water is used in washing dishes, taking baths, or flushing toilets, it heads to the wastewater facility to become clean and usable again. Once there, water goes through a rigorous process involving a variety of machines and chemicals to remove the waste, kill harmful bacteria, and purify it before it is deemed safe enough for reuse.

Who does all this cleaning and testing? Wastewater technicians! They are trained to operate the water treatment equipment, read meters and gauges that control the chemicals used to purify water, and maintain the systems that get water to and from the plant. They are ultimately respon-

What Do You Think?

What do you think would happen if the whole world flushed the toilet at the same time?

WOW!

The earth is 80 percent water, but only 1 percent is drinkable for humans and animals.

You want to make a big splash in life.

Just cleaning out the cat's litter box (or scooping your dog's poop) is enough to make you puke.

sible for the safety of the water used in hundreds, thousands, and sometimes millions of homes. It's a big responsibility!

If you think your school bathroom gets stinky, can you even imagine what the waste from an entire town smells like? Of course, you'd probably rather not. Unpleasant odors are one of the obvious occupational hazards associated with this job. Of course, there are times when wastewater technicians have to get uncomfortably close to huge vats of waste in order to conduct tests and make repairs. They're extra careful at these times, because one wrong move and they could be taking the ultimate swirly!

Go Online to Find Out More!

Find out more than you ever wanted to know about sewage at http://www.sandiego.gov/mwwd/kids.

Gross Job #10

Zookeeper

A zookeeper works with a sloth during the annual head count of more than 600 species at the London Zoo. *Cathal McNaughton/ AP Wire*

Zookeepers sometimes get a bum rap. Some people seem to think that all they do is scoop poop and clean out cages. Sure, that's part of the job. But after you do it for awhile, it's no big deal, and it's really just one of many tasks on a zookeeper's daily to-do list.

The most important task for zookeepers—whether they are responsible for gorillas or giraffes—is to protect and care for wild animals in zoos and animal parks. They pay special attention to feeding animals carefully planned meals tailored especially to the nutritional needs of each species (like dishing out up to 40 pounds of raw meat for a tiger's dinner). They work with other experts to create and maintain comfortable living spaces that are as close to each type of animal's natural habitat as

What Do You Think?
What if people and animals could change places? What kind of zoos do you think animals would keep people in?

possible. They also closely monitor each animal's health and work with veterinarians to address any health care needs. Sometimes they even administer medicine to animals when they are sick! Imagine telling a polar bear to "be a good boy and take your medicine!"

Zookeepers may spend time training some animals or making sure others get adequate exercise. Contrary to popular opinion, a zookeeper's job is not all fun and games (and poop!). Zookeepers rarely get to play with the animals they protect. The animals are wild, after all! They do tend to form special bonds with their creatures, though, and they get to know the habits and preferences of the animals very well.

This knowledge comes in handy when zookeepers are asked to give tours of the zoo or to talk in classrooms to students about their work. For those students wanting a more hands-on experience in zookeeping, many zoos provide junior zookeeper classes where kids can perform the same jobs that zookeepers do in real life.

Variety is not only one of the best things about a zoo; it's also one of the best things about a zookeeper's work. Many zookeepers specialize in a favorite type of animal, such as reptiles, nocturnal animals, or primates. Some even work in aquariums with otters, penguins, and (gulp!) sharks!

WOW!

Almost one in four of the animals at the National Zoo in Washington, D.C., is considered an endangered species, including giant pandas, Asian elephants, white-naped cranes, and western lowland gorillas.

You are a magnet for stray animals.

You aren't totally, completely crazy in love with animals.

Most zookeepers will tell you that no two days are alike when it comes to taking care of the wild kingdom.

Zookeeping is one of those rare jobs that actually is as fun as it sounds. So, it should come as no surprise to discover that zookeeping is one of the most competitive jobs around! There are often more people wanting to be zookeepers than there are zookeeper jobs. In order to qualify, zookeepers must attend college for at least two to four years, learning all they can about animal science.

Go Online to Find Out More!

Build a home for your very own tiger at http://www.nationalgeographic.com/tigers/maina.html.

More Gross Jobs

Ready to get grossed out some more? One thing is for sure: The following jobs aren't for sissies. But even if you don't want to do them yourself, you have to be glad that someone else has the guts (and the strong stomach) to do what it takes to get these jobs done.

Autopsy Technician

When someone dies and no one knows why, they are sent to the coroner's office for an autopsy. Autopsies are medical procedures that involve investigating a dead body—inside and out—for clues to determine the cause of death. Forensic pathologists are doctors in charge of performing autopsies, and autopsy technicians are the assistants who help. In other words, they get stuck doing all the things the forensic pathologist doesn't want to do, like prepping dead bodies for the autopsy, taking photographs of the body and various organs, and handling specimens of bodily fluids needed for testing.

When things in the lab get a little too gross, there are still discussions with funeral home directors to be had and loads of paperwork to complete. And, of course, there is always the satisfaction of knowing that your efforts have helped someone who was unable to help himself or herself.

Butcher

Spoiler alert! The following information might ruin your appetite!

Remember when you were a little kid and you made your first visit to a farm? If you are like a lot of other clueless little kids, that was where you first discovered the connection between the chicken nuggets you liked to eat and the cute little chicks pecking their way around the barn.

Not to make a bad situation even worse, but before those chicken nuggets end up in Happy Meals around the world, they (and their beef and pork counterparts) spend some time on a butcher's counter getting sliced and diced into the various "cuts" that people use to make meals. Even though it's easier—and a lot more pleasant—to pretend that the meat people eat just comes in neatly packaged portions, the truth is someone has to do unthinkable things to it before it's ready for human consumption. That *someone* is a butcher, who uses precise procedures and tools like knives and saws and meat hooks to get the job done.

Port-A-Potty Servicer

Most people won't go near these places unless it's an absolute "gotta go" emergency. Make a career out of cleaning them? You've got to be kidding. The "places" in question are called port-a-potties or portable toilets. We've all used port-a-potties before, while camping or watching a parade or having fun at a fair. We've all yelled, "Gross!" when we went inside, tried really hard not to look down, and—especially important—did our best to hold our breath until the deed was done.

If you think it's bad to use a port-a-potty once in a while, just imagine what it must be like to have to clean them all the time! It's the ultimate pooper-scooper experience! Large tank trucks roll up and the cleaners use vacuums connected to the truck to simply suck each port-a-potty dry. Fun, huh? They repeat this process until the day is done and then empty the waste-filled truck to a sewage facility. But, here's the real question: Who has to clean the truck?

Restaurant Dishwasher

Do you complain about having to do your family's dinner dishes? Can you imagine what it would be like to spend eight hours a day washing dishes that strangers have used to eat meals in a restaurant? Make that dish after dish after dish...

In busy restaurants and cafes around the world, that's exactly what dishwashers do—hundreds and thousands of times a day. Fortunately, they usually get help you don't get at home in the form of professional-quality equipment that quickly cleans, sanitizes, and dries even the worst kinds of stains. But there is no getting around the fact that this job is hot, messy, and, quite frankly, kind of gross.

If you think your mom or dad gets mad when you don't do it right, you don't even want to know how a restaurant dishwasher feels—just try serving a paying customer with a crumb-crusted fork or lipstick-smeared glass. Professional dishwashing is yet another example of a job that nobody seems to notice until it's not done right.

Roadkill Cleaner

Did you hear the one about "Why did the chicken cross the road?" Well, in this case, the chicken didn't make it, and it's no joke that the roadkill cleaner had to be called in to clean up the mess.

In case you're wondering, roadkill cleaners do pretty much what their job title says—they clean up animals that have met unfortunate ends at the wrong end of a motorized vehicle. It might be a couple of dogs and a deer one day and a bear, a half-dozen squirrels, and even a skunk (phew!) the next day. As you might imagine (and have probably seen for yourself a time or two), roadkill is not a pretty sight. Cleaners come in trucks and take the dead creatures to the nearest landfill for, if not a proper burial, a proper disposal.

Roughneck

Looking for a job that's noisy, dirty, dangerous, and located somewhere in the middle of an ocean? Well, you have to look no further than your nearest offshore oil rig. Offshore oilrigs are special platforms used to drill oil and are located wherever oil is found and can be extracted with a minimum disturbance to the environment. Translated, that usually means in remote locations, far away from places where most people work and live. Roughnecks are part of the crew that cleans the rigs, maintains the equipment, and does other manual labor tasks.

Not only do roughnecks tend to work long hours, but they also spend long periods of time living on the oil rig that they're working on. It's simply too far away from land to commute back and forth on a regular basis. That's the bad news. The good news is that they tend to work for a concentrated period, say six to eight weeks, and then they get an extended period off. They make good money too: upwards of $100,000 once they've gotten some experience and moved into a supervisory position. Rigs are built on super-strong platforms permanently anchored onto the ocean floor, equipped with drilling and production equipment and living quarters for crewmembers.

Sewer Inspector

If you've ever wondered what happens after you flush the toilet or wash something down a sink's drain, just ask a sewer inspector. They know only too well what happens to the billions of gallons of wastewater running through the endless maze of sewer pipes beneath every big city and tiny town known to civilized society. They know because they are the ones who open up manhole covers and actually go down into sewers when there are problems that need to be fixed.

Wait a second! Is it really true that sewer inspectors willingly go underground into pipes filled with all kinds of stinky, yucky stuff? Yes, and did we mention that, because of the size of the pipes, they often have to crawl on all fours to get to where they are going? Of course, they wear chest-high waders, so no big deal, right? They say you eventually get used to the smell. But the rats and roaches you often encounter down below are another story.

Underwear Inspector

Everybody wears them. Somebody has to make them. And, thank heavens, somebody else makes sure that they get made right. Nobody likes getting their knickers in a knot, so underwear inspectors make sure that each unmentionable has the proper comfort, fit, and absorbency.

So essentially, underwear inspectors spend their days looking at other people's undies. Fortunately, the garments are clean.... But if you think this is gross, you probably don't want to hear about the people who test underwear for its resistance to flatulent smells (meaning stinky farts).

Real People, Gross Jobs

What one person may consider to be a gross job another person may consider a golden opportunity. That is certainly true for the following people. Read on to find out more about the unusual challenges they tackle on the job.

PEOPLE PROFILE #1: Lyle Estill, Biofuels Manufacturer

"You give me fat, and I'll give you fuel," says biofuels manufacturer Lyle Estill. He is leading the way in alternative energy by using animal fats and vegetable oils instead of diesel fuel to power cars and trucks. According to Estill, we are using up the last of the world's oil, so he is trying to figure out a way to keep us going in the years ahead.

Estill was just an ordinary guy who liked to recycle, but one day he deep-fried a turkey and it changed his life forever. Deep-fried turkeys sure are tasty, but they leave a lot of goopy oil in the bottom of the pot with nowhere to go. Instead of just tossing out the oil like most people, Estill realized that he could also recycle it. Before he knew it, Estill was fueling his tractor on biodiesel he made from used cooking oil!

After taking a class on biofuels at a local college, Estill and his friends began building bigger and bigger biofuel processors. Pretty soon, they weren't just filling up Estill's tractor—they were running cars, trucks, and other machines on biofuels! From that deep-fried turkey Estill has created Piedmont Biofuels, the largest biofuels cooperative in the United States. The company ships more than 7,600 gallons of biofuel every other day!

But they can't make 7,600 gallons from recycled cooking oil alone, can they? Nope—Estill and his company are constantly experimenting with alternative fuel sources like soybeans and canola. In fact, they are one of the first companies in the world to use chicken fat as a biofuel! There might be a reason not everyone is doing it, however—chicken fat is messy! Lyle says the dirtiest part of his job is having to clean up after a spill, from chicken fat to biodiesel to glycerin. It's all worth it in the end, though. Thanks to Estill and Piedmont Biofuels, we'll be driving for a very long time!

PEOPLE PROFILE #2: Michael L. Fox, Wastewater Treatment and Collection Supervisor

If you ever happen to go to the bathroom in Conover, North Carolina, you won't have to wonder where your "waste" goes. It goes straight to a waste-water treatment plant supervised by Michael L. Fox. He makes sure the wastewater from the businesses and 6,000 residents of Conover is clean before releasing it back into the environment. Fox bets that you can't guess what he uses to clean it up. (Here's a clue: It's something that, at first glance, might seem kind of gross and even a little dangerous.)

And the answer is...Bacteria! Surprised? If you are like most people, when you think of bacteria, you think of germs or disease and, for the most part, you'd be correct. But Fox says that a certain kind of bacteria actually eats the pollution and eliminates the waste. Fox explains that, since this type of bacteria multiplies and dies quickly, technicians constantly remove old bacteria to make room for young, strong bacteria to grow. The removed bacteria are called sludge, and it is eventually used safely as fertilizer or compost after all the bacteria has been killed. Before water goes back out for use in the community, technicians add chlorine and other chemicals to it to kill bacteria and make it safe for fragile ecosystems.

What's the grossest part of the job? Fox says it's the grates. Since bacteria can't break down materials like plastics, paper, or wood that find their way into the water, grates and other equipment at the plant catch all the solid crud. Unfortunately, there's only one way to get rid of it and that's for a person to clean it. Ugh!

And what about the smell? Fox says you just get used to it after awhile.

PEOPLE PROFILE #3: Judith Gordon, Forensic Services Director

Judith Gordon is the "boss" of the criminal investigation unit for the Charleston Police Department in South Carolina. That means she heads up a staff of 23 people, which includes crime scene investigators who collect and document evidence, crime scene photographers who take photos of actual crime scenes, latent print experts who work with fingerprint evidence, crime lab scientists who analyze physical evidence, polygraph experts who administer lie detector tests, and digital evidence experts who gather evidence from technology like cell phones and computers.

She started out as a scientist herself—working in a crime lab testing drugs, blood, body fluids, and evidence from suspicious fires. Now she manages the work her staff does on about 10,000 criminal cases a year.

These days she only goes out to investigate big cases that involve homicide, big fires, or some other unique aspect. Gordon admits that it was really hard the first time she saw a dead body, and it still isn't easy. But now she finds it can be harder to deal with the survivors. She recalls a case where a mother and child were killed and says the worst part was witnessing the father's grief when he found out what happened.

Gordon is especially excited about technological breakthroughs like DNA testing and the national fingerprint database that they can use to get more answers from their evidence. She is currently reviewing files from 50 cold murder cases dating back as far as 1980 to see if the evidence they've carefully preserved can be used to identify the murderers.

PEOPLE PROFILE #4: Kathy Reichs, Forensic Anthropologist and Author

When Kathy Reichs was your age, she already knew she wanted to be a scientist. At the time, she pictured herself wearing "a white lab coat and squinting into a microscope." Little did she know back then that she would someday become a world-famous forensic anthropologist.

Reichs started out working with old bones as a bio-archaeologist. She says she was lured to forensics by police officers bringing cases to her lab. She had to go back to school for training in this specialty, but eventually became one of only 70 scientists certified by the American Board of Forensic Anthropology.

Now, it's hard to say if Reichs is more famous for her work as a forensic anthropologist or as author of a best-selling series of books about—you guessed it—a forensic anthropologist named Temperance Brennan or as the inspiration behind the Fox television series *Bones*. Most people would find working for both the Office of the Chief Medical Examiner in North Carolina and for the Laboratoire de Sciences Judiciaires et de Medecine Legale for the province of Quebec in Canada enough of a challenge. It's in those roles that she's handled cases as demanding as identifying victims' remains at Ground Zero following the 9/11 World Trade Center terrorist attack and as diverse as verifying the ancient remains of a women whom the Vatican was considering for sainthood.

But simply working cases like these is not enough for Reichs. She likes to write about them too—often finding the thread of an idea in an actual case and weaving a fictional, spellbinding story from there.

Gross Job Playground

You've read about gross jobs that other people do. Here's your chance to play around with the idea of having a gross job yourself someday. So, what do you think? Could you do it? Would you dare? (Oh, and by the way, if this book doesn't belong to you, please use a separate sheet of paper.)

Watch Out, Gross Job, Here I Come

First, imagine that you're all grown up, and ready to tackle a gross career...

Would You Do It?	Can't Wait to Try It Someday!	Maybe—If I Ever Get The Nerve!	Not A Chance!
Crime Scene Investigator			
Exterminator			
Forensic Anthropologist			
Infectious Disease Scientist			
Janitor			
Landfill Manager			
Mortician			
Plumber			
Wastewater Technician			
Zookeeper			

Mirror, Mirror on the Wall...

Which of these jobs is grossest of them all?

- Autopsy Technician
- Butcher
- Port-a-Potty Servicer
- Restaurant Dishwasher
- Roadkill Cleaner
- Roughneck
- Sewer Inspector
- Underwear Inspector

Help Wanted: Tough Person for a Really Gross Job

Pick one of the gross jobs listed above and pretend that someone has just quit, leaving you in charge to hire a replacement. It's a tough job, but somebody has to do it! So quick, make up an ad that will convince some brave soul to take it on. Be sure to weed out the weak-kneed riffraff by emphasizing the special "talents" it takes to get the job done.

Hot Off the Press!

What's your idea of an absolutely gross job? Can you invent one so totally disgusting that people everywhere will cringe when they read about it?

Pretend that the editor of a wacky magazine thinks your job is so weird that he wants to feature you on the front cover. He asked you to write a short story about what you do. Include tons of behind-the-scenes information, and don't be afraid to gross things up with all the gory details.

One More Thing...

Here's some room to list any good books or interesting Web sites you find to further explore gross job ideas. You can use a search engine like http://kids.yahoo.com to search for information by typing in the name of a career you'd like to know more about. Or ask your school media specialist or librarian for help in finding some books.

Index

Note: **Bold** page numbers indicate a photo.